MAKING MGs

Other books of interest to enthusiasts available from Veloce -

Alfa Romeo, How to Power Tune Alfa Romeo Twin-Cam Engines (Speedpro Series)
by Jim Kartalamakis
Alfa Romeo Giulia Coupe GT & GTA
by John Tipler
Alfa Romeo Modello 8C 2300
by Angela Cherrett
Alfa Romeo Owner's Bible
by Pat Braden
Biggles!
by Peter Berresford Ellis & Jennifer Schofield
Bubblecars & Microcars: Colour Family Album
by Andrea & David Sparrow
Big Bugattis - Types 46 & 50
by Barrie Price
Bugatti 57 - The Last French Bugatti
by Barrie Price
Car Bodywork & Interior: Care & Repair
by David Pollard
Citroen 2CV: Colour Family Album
by Andrea & David Sparrow
Citroen DS: Colour Family Album
by Andrea & David Sparrow
Cobra: The Real Thing!
by Trevor Legate
Completely Morgan: Four-Wheelers 1936-1968
by Ken Hill
Completely Morgan: Four-Wheelers from 1968
by Ken Hill
Daimler SP250 'Dart'
by Brian Long
Fiat & Abarth 124 Spider & Coupe
by John Tipler
Fiat & Abarth 500 & 600
by Malcolm Bobbitt
Lola T70
by John Starkey
Mazda MX5/Miata Enthusiast's Workshop Manual
by Rod Grainger & Pete Shoemark
MGB, How to give your MGB V8 Power (Speedpro Series)
by Roger Williams
Mini Cooper: The Real Thing!
by John Tipler
Motorcycling in the 50s
by Jeff Clew
Nuvolari: When Nuvolari Raced ...
by Valerio Moretti
Pass the MoT
by David Pollard
Rover P4 Series (60•75•80•90•95•100•105•110)
by Malcolm Bobbitt

First published in 1995 by Veloce Publishing Plc., Godmanstone, Dorset DT2 7AE, England. Fax 01300 341065

ISBN 1 874105 53 7

Readers with ideas for automotive books, or books on other transport or related hobby subjects are invited to write to the editorial director of Veloce Publishing at the above address.

British Library Cataloguing in Publication Data -
A catalogue record for this book is available from the British Library.

Typesetting (Suotane), design and page make-up all by Veloce on Apple Mac.

Printed and bound in England

VELOCE AUTO-ARCHIVE SERIES

MAKING MGs

John Price Williams

VELOCE PUBLISHING PLC
PUBLISHERS OF FINE AUTOMOTIVE BOOKS

Acknowledgements

I have always been fascinated by car factories, particularly those making sports cars, and, fortunately, many people have shared my enthusiasm and been remarkably helpful during research into this book, including several who worked at Abingdon and who are named in the text.

Other than those, I would like to thank in particular the British Motor Industry Heritage Trust; books like this could not be written without the estimable work done by the Trust, especially by its research archivist, Anders Clausager, who has given permission for the use of MG production figures; the Trust's photographic assistant, Karam Ram was also most helpful in providing some of the valuable pictures.

Many thanks are due also for permission to use pictures, which came from Roche Bentley and Richard Monk of the MG Owners' Club; Paddy Willmer and Colin Light of the MG Car Club; John Brigden who provided the Heritage pictures; John Digby, formerly of BL; Mike Ellman-Brown for his outstanding sequence of the building of his twin-cam; Ian Smith; Carol Page of *Classic and Sportscar*; Annice Collett at the library of the National Motor Museum at Beaulieu; Gordon Horne of Motor Panels and Kevin Jones and Vincent Hammersley of the Rover Group. Tim Blott, editor of the *Oxford Mail*, kindly gave permission for the use of pictures from the newspaper group's library which has many shots of the Abingdon years taken by their own photographers. Mike Allison, an MG expert who worked at Abingdon, kindly checked the proofs.

Finally, thanks to Rod Grainger of Veloce Publishing who thought a series on car factories was a project worth pursuing.

John Price Williams
Eastbourne

Contents

Introduction

It was the biggest and the best sports car factory in the world. Abingdon-on-Thames, the small Berkshire town - now in Oxfordshire - produced more sports cars than any other place, earning an outstanding reputation which remains to this day. The remnants of the works have become a place of pilgrimage as well as headquarters of the MG Car Club.

The factory was never a car manufacturing plant, for its role was always to assemble components made by others; firstly as part of the Nuffield empire and later as a member of the British Motor Corporation and the ill-fated Leyland group. However, it did contain design and competitions departments which were to play a major role in the success of MG.

The move to Abingdon from Oxford was made in 1929 when MG outgrew the works at Edmund Road, Cowley and a factory was bought at Abingdon. This consisted of the disused part of the Pavlova leather works, which had done huge business during the first world war making, among other things, sheepskin coats for the armed forces. The unusual name was bestowed by a director of the company who admired the ballerina.

The remarkable thing about the fifty years of MG production that took place there was that cars were made in almost exactly the same way at the beginning in the twenties until production end in the eighties. Robot welders, powered tracks and streams of conveyors were unknown. Bodies were lowered on to chassis through a hole in the floor and then pushed along the line until completion: until the 1970s each car was given a proper road test before despatch. By

the end of the thirties the works was making 2500 cars a year; when production resumed after the war using, in addition, a factory built for making tanks, production began rising steadily to 20,000 and eventually 50,000 cars a year. Not all of these, of course, were MGs. Austin-Healeys (the 3000 and the Sprite), Rileys and even Morris Minor Travellers and vans were assembled there, but the sign on the gate said "MG".

Between the wars, MG made a large and bewildering range of models, one of the most important being the M-type Midget of 1928-32, which had the Morris Minor chassis and body by Carbodies of Coventry. This set the style for the small two-seater sports car for which MG was to become world-renowned. The J-type which followed, and then the PA and PB leading to the TA and TB, all followed the same theme. But there were also stylish saloons, like the KN Magnette of 1934, and then the big SA and WA range, powered by six-cylinder engines of 2288 and 2561ccs.

Midget bodies, by the late thirties, were made at Morris Motors body plant in Coventry and delivered to Abingdon as an ash-framed centre section which was then assembled to the chassis. Many of the more expensive cars, however, had specialist bodies made by Tickford and Charlesworth.

The rationalisation of the Morris, Wolseley and MG empire into the

Still a cottage industry. An TD Midget has its body (from the Morris Bodies branch in Coventry) lowered on to the chassis at Abingdon. Production of the TD peaked in 1952, when almost 11,000 examples were built.

Making MGs

Nuffield group in 1935 led not only to the closure of the design office at Abingdon and withdrawal from racing, but also to the adaption of standard production engines from within the group, which set the pattern for the next 45 years.

When war broke out, the factory was producing some 1000 Midgets a year and, when it was all over, MG went back into production with the TC Midget, substantially the same car as the pre-war TB. Production quickly began to exceed pre-war rates, building to 3000 cars a year by 1948. By now, the factory was also building the neat Y-type saloon and tourer, based on the Morris 8 series E body, which sported a de-tuned version of the TC's 1250cc XPAG engine. It was the first Nuffield car with rack and pinion steering and independent front suspension; features which were carried over to the MGA.

As the benefits of scale of the Nuffield merger worked though and materials became more readily available, production went on climbing. With the "export or die" philosophy of the late forties and early fifties came the first major success in overseas markets for MG, as 24,000 examples of the TC's successor, the TD, were sold in four years in the United States. Again, this established a pattern for the future, with huge quantities of sports cars going from Abingdon to America until the end of production in 1980.

What this book aims to show is not only the processes that went into making the world's favourite sports cars in this important period from the fifties (when mass-production began), to the regrettable day when the factory gates closed for the last time, but also how the name MG has been kept alive ever since by successors to those original classic cars.

MGA - the first mass-produced MG

The small Thames-side town of Abingdon experienced a bustle in the mid-fifties like never before as scores of lorries from all over the Midlands poured into the marshalling area of the MG works, waiting their turn to be directed by a system of coloured lights which summoned them to unload into the factory.

Production of 8800 cars a year in 1954 was to soar to 27,500 by 1957. Abingdon was producing more cars in one year than it produced in the entire ten-year period from the opening of the factory in 1929 to the outbreak of war. It became the home of the British Motor Corporation sports car division, producing not only MGs but also the big Austin-Healey 100. But the major reason for the huge production boost was the introduction of the MGA, an outstanding sports car, more than 100,000 of which were sold.

And why 'A'? Simply, 'Z' had been used for the Magnette and, as the general manager, John Thornley, was to write: "It compels the use of the name MG whenever reference is made to it and, what's more, 25 further models can be produced before the same problem recurs"!

As befits a proper sports car, the MGA had its genesis in racing. In 1949 and 1950, *Autocar* photographer George Phillips raced at Le Mans in his own version of the MG TC and, for the following year, he persuaded Sydney Enever to build him a new streamlined body, mounted on the TD chassis which had, for the first time for an MG sports car, independent front suspension and rack and pinion steering. It was powered by a race-tuned version of the familiar 1250cc XPAG engine and could attain 120mph.

MG special projects were given EX prefixes and a number and this car became EX172, known better by its registration number of UMG 400. Although a broken valve put Phillips out of the 1952 race, this one-off special was greatly influential, since the low, smooth profile of the body, reminiscent of the Jaguar XK120, was remarkably like the MGA which was to go into production three years later.

The next step came when Enever decided that the seating position in EX172 was too high, since the seat was on top of the chassis. To lower it, he designed a completely new chassis, moving the seat down between the chassis rail and the transmission tunnel. This chassis - again - was to be most significant and two cars were built at Abingdon; EX175, designed as a production sports car, and EX179, the streamlined car used by Capt. George Eyston and the American Ken Miles on the Utah salt flats in 1954 when they broke several records at speeds of up to 154mph.

EX175, registered HMO 6, was not a true MGA prototype since it had the MG TF engine of 1466cc, but it fixed the body lines of the MGA almost precisely, though it was another two years before sanction for its production was granted, the process being delayed by internal rivalries in BMC, which was heavily Austin-biased

But the prowess of the tiny design team at Abingdon, coupled with falling sales of the TF which received a lukewarm reception at its introduction in 1953 where it was memorably described as "looking like a TD which had been kicked in the face", finally persuaded the heads of BMC that the MG factory could produce a new model. In 1954 permission was given for a proper design team to be based at Abingdon - after a break of nearly 20 years - to build the first new MG sports car since the TA Midget of 1936.

The target date for introduction of the new car was April 1955. In common with the ZA Magnette already being made at Abingdon, it was to have BMC mechanicals, notably the B-series 1498cc engine. To increase power, two larger semi-downdraught SU carburettors, a different camshaft, stronger valve springs and different manifolds were fitted which, in the first cars, gave 68bhp at 5500rpm.

The gearbox and hypoid bevel axle also came from the B-series range, being manufactured at the Tractor and Transmissions division at Ward End, Birmingham. The clutch came from Borg and Beck and the propeller shaft from Hardy Spicer.

Unlike the Magnette, the MGA was to have a sturdy separate chassis, just like every other MG sports car. This was becoming something of an anachronism, since most manufacturers were switching to unitary construction: one-piece body/chassis shells on to which the mechanicals were bolted.

The body was engineered by Morris Bodies in Coventry and panels made by Pressed Steel, who failed to provide them to meet the April target date because they had experimented with plastic dies to form the body panels. The

Making MGs

experiment was not a success and there was a delay while production reverted to the use of steel dies.

The delay was embarrassing but smoothed over by the appearance at Le Mans in June of three MGA prototypes of type EX182, which ran successfully even though one crashed. Four cars were driven there by mechanics, but only three ran.

Their highly-tuned B-series engines could produce 120mph with driver-only up; the bodies, built at Abingdon and consisting of 18-gauge alloy panels held

Production of the MGA was delayed because of press tool problems, and these alloy-bodied cars, hand-built at Abingdon, are seen setting out for Le Mans in June 1955; the car's first public outing. Only three of the cars ran as one was intended as a spare and, although one car crashed, the other two finished strongly. The race was completely overshadowed, however, by catastrophe when a Mercedes plunged into the grandstand, killing more than 80 people.

by countersunk rivets to the frame, followed closely the style of the soon-to-be-introduced production car.

The motoring press, which, in those days, adhered to embargo dates for the announcement of new cars, was allowed to hint that the production cars were on the way and *Autosport* reported presciently that when this happened "the rustle of cheques being signed will be heard throughout the world".

Testing of the production prototypes went on at MIRA at Lindley on track, ripple surfaces and in the dust tunnel. The testers also used an airfield at nearby Halfpenny Green for skid-pan experiments. Suspension and tyre tests were also done later at the Dunlop track, and the results were said to have led to modifications which added 3mph to the car's top speed. Compared with the MG TF, with its 57bhp and top speed of 85mph, the new MGA developed, at first, 68bhp and, later, 72bhp and hit 98mph.

The first production MGA began going down the line at Abingdon on May

16 1955 and the first to leave the factory was despatched on July 13 of that year. The car's debut was at the Frankfurt motor show.

The decision had been taken that the MGA would be a mass-produced sports car, rather than a hand-built one, which meant that, because of space restrictions at Abingdon, large components would be fabricated in other factories and then brought to MG for assembly. The body - although not an integral chassis/body unit - was a substantial construction, delivered to the factory with all the main panels welded in. Wings came separately, on occasion, to be bolted on, and were finished by panel beaters and sprayed before attachment. Doors, bonnet and boot lid, added later, were skinned with aluminium.

The bodies - painted and trimmed - arrived from Coventry in big, open, double-decker transporters, three up and three down. They were unloaded on the first floor - 'top deck' as it was known - and mounted on four-wheel trolleys and

pushed along as Lucas electrical equipment and other components were added. Unlike today's 'just in time' processes of car manufacture, where components arrive at the factory only when they are needed, there were some stocks of spare bodies held at the works, usually up to a day's production, in case of delivery delays from Cowley caused by industrial action. However, each body took up almost as much room as a complete car and space at the factory was limited.

The trim came from various manufacturers; the ICI Vynide hoods from Coventry Hood and Seating (changed to Wardle's Everflex from the 1600 onwards), sidescreens by Weathershields, seats were in Connolly's Celstra leather on the wearing surfaces, later changed to Vaumol, and the carpets - nearly all black - were Crossley's Carvel.

Meanwhile, on the floor below, the chassis was taking shape, built up from box-section sidemembers, tubular crossmembers and the most important

Making MGs

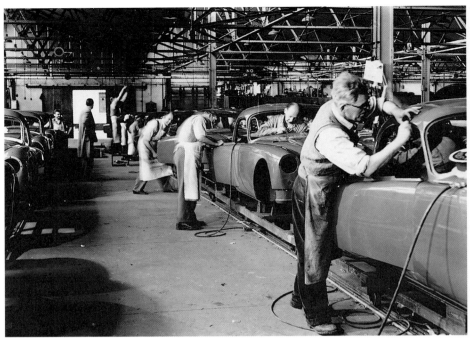

'goal post' structure which kept the scuttle rigid. The components came from John Thompson of Wolverhampton and were largely made of heavy 14-gauge steel.

The weight of the chassis was often criticised by those who thought that a lighter unit would have made a faster car, but Sydney Enever retorted that the chassis could rust away two thicknesses and the MGA would still be a good safe car to have a 'shunt' in. And Roy Brocklehurst, who was to succeed him, described it as probably the best separate chassis frame ever engineered.

Welding of the chassis took place on rotary jigs, then a overhead conveyor dipped the complete unit into a bath of stove enamel; it was left dripping for a while and then fired in an infra-red oven for six minutes.

The next step was adding the front and rear suspension pressings and the Dunlop wheels and tyres. As many as 60% of customers specified wire wheels, much to the bewilderment of MG management, who had long considered them an anachronism and their pierced wheels elegant enough.

The chassis began its progress down the production line, being pushed by hand along a pair of raised tracks, just as in the 1930s. Then the tracks were wood and steel; after the war they were made of breeze-blocks incorporating a metal channel in which the left-hand wheels could run while the right-hand wheels were on a flat surface. In this way the lines could accommodate cars of different track widths. Then the body descended from the first floor through a hole in the floor for mounting on the chassis. The coupe already had its fixed head, which had been welded on at the body plant. In trim, the main differences between it and the roadster were its wind-up windows and exterior door handles.

The B-series engine, made at Longbridge, was run-in there electrically with the sump off before being delivered

Though most bodies arrived at the works already painted, some spraying was done at Abingdon on occasion. Here, in November 1961, a tourer body is being painted white, the most popular colour.

The B-series engine, with carburettors and manifolds already attached, is inserted into the chassis. Note the substantial nature of the 'goalpost'.

The body is lowered from the 'top deck', with electrics in place, to be mated with the chassis.

The special bonnet prop holds open the lid as the heater controls are attached.

to Abingdon, where it was dropped in from an Ardegar hoist. Manifolds were added here with the SU carburettors, engine mounting rubbers and the remote control casting for the gearbox.

Each car coming down the line had a note on the windscreen specifying the type of wheels, lamps and speedometer needed and whether the car was to be fitted with the left- or right-hand Cam Gears rack and pinion system inherited from the TF. The specification was de-

Making MGs

Below: An inspector checks the underside before the road test. Loose suspension mountings were a common fault which caused cars to be returned for rectification.

cided by the planning department, who analysed customer orders. White was the most popular colour and, with variations in the fitting of steering, heaters, wheels and radios, only about two cars in every 500 were exactly the same.

Not every car ended up as it should be, however: Henry Stone recalled that, in his time at Abingdon, he had seen a right-hand drive car coming off the line with the pedals on the left and another with wire wheels on the front and disc wheels on the back!

At the end of the line lights were checked and steering tracked on a Weaver machine before drivers took each car on a six mile road test; an MG tradition which persisted up until the 1970s.

The rectification department dealt with faults of a mechanical nature and in paintwork, each being noted in a log-book made out of the chassis and body card. About 15 cars an hour were going through this process in 1957, according to *Motor Sport*, which visited the works to chronicle the MGA's progress.

Faults in the finish were marked with chalk rings and retouched or polished out under neon strip lights before a final wash and polish passed the cars fit to leave the works. Cars destined for export - which meant most of them - were covered with protective wax.

Owners who wished to pick up their

Above: In the 1950s you were allowed to collect your own car from the factory. Mike Ellman-Brown's 1500 gets a final polish in the despatch department. The building of Mike's MGA twin-cam, which followed his 1500, is detailed in a later chapter.

Right: Waiting for its final check with the production specifications still attached to the windscreen.

Left: The factory allowed owners to fill up with four gallons of Premium petrol for the journey home.

Below: A security guard checks the chassis number against the release paperwork before allowing the car to leave the factory.

Making MGs

The spring of 1959, left to right: the first MG ,"Old No 1", bearing an incorrect 1950 Berkshire registration number, a 1936 PB and a 1500 tourer. Behind are MGs destined for America and, in the background, Austin-Healey Sprites and 100/6 models awaiting despatch.

own cars from the factory were allowed to do so, but the great majority were ferried by teams of drivers to the marshalling bays 13 miles away at Cowley, the drivers returning by bus to pick up more cars. And so it went on, day after day, reaching a record output of nearly 23,500 MGAs in 1959, produced by a staff of just over 1000.

As John Thornley pointed out, if you took away the 300 or so people needed for administration, the output of cars per worker was phenomenally high, though that, of course, was mainly due to the fact that large sub-assemblies were made elsewhere and delivered ready-to-fit.

Magnette - the
sporting saloon

MG owners, more than most, are quite ready to be outraged at slights, imagined or otherwise, to the marque. There was, therefore, some exasperation expressed when, in 1953, a brand-new MG saloon - the Magnette - was announced.

The cause of the perturbation was two-fold: firstly, those with short memories thought that MG should be building only sports cars, forgetting - or not knowing - of the distinguished line of sporting saloons that Abingdon had produced from the 1934 KN Magnette to the VA in 1939 (the petite MG Y-series saloons, based on the Morris 8 series E body, were not really taken seriously by *aficionados*). Secondly, the car, code-named ZA, had a new 1.5-litre engine, which was not going to go into the current sports car, the TF, announced at the same time. Even *this* car's reception, as has been noted, was less than enthusiastic because it was yet another warmed-over version of the pre-war Midget, with the same old 1250cc XPAG engine.

Those who objected were not to know that much more exciting developments were about to take place at Abingdon and on the track. In the meantime, the new Magnette, designed by Gerald Palmer, produced a couple of firsts: it was the first MG produced without a chassis, utilising unit construction, and it was the first car to use the new 1489cc power unit developed as a result of the merger of Nuffield and Austin into BMC though, in fact, the basis of the engine could be traced back to the Austin 10 of 1932. Other major parts common to the BMC empire were the gearbox and rear axle.

This B-series engine, as it was known

and once described by one of its designers as "horrible", was to serve MG - and BMC - very well for nearly 30 years. It was also, compared with earlier MG engines, reasonably oil-tight. Twin SU carburettors gave it a respectable 60bhp, compared with 46bhp for the Y-type it replaced.

And why was this engine not in the TF? "Actually," confided *Motor* " the unit is still in fairly small production and it is not yet possible to build it in sufficient quantity for the large output of Midgets."

The body, which had overtones of the Lancia Aurelia, was made by Pressed Steel at Cowley and was not entirely new, since it was similar to the Wolseley 4/44 announced the previous year, though, confusingly, that car was still using a single carburettor version of the 1250cc MG Midget engine. This was because both the Wolseley and the Magnette had originally been designed by Palmer to take MG/Morris parts. But when the BMC merger took place, the Magnette, still in planning stage, was redesigned to take the Austin-built engine.

The body arrived painted, but only

The first MG to be engined by Austin, the Magnette was also the first BMC car to use the B-series engine, which then soldiered on for nearly 30 years in various models, most notably, of course, the MGB. This factory shot, taken in front of a large piece of plywood with a Magnette just visible behind, shows the neat inlet manifold bearing the MG octagon. (Courtesy BMIHT/Rover Group)

Left: In the spring of 1956 an MGA 1500 poses in front of Magnette shells waiting to be delivered to the top deck for trimming. A fine array of Abingdon products - including Rileys - make up the background. (Courtesy BMIHT/Rover Group)

as a shell. It was finished and trimmed on the first floor, and it was there also that the engine was fitted. Two workers manoeuvred it in with an overhead crane, with a production rate of one every 20 minutes. The exhaust pipe and 4.55:1 B-series back axle were fitted. Suspension was independent at the front, a revised version of the wishbones used in the Y-type, and the crossmember which carried it, fabricated by John Thompson's works at Wolverhampton, was jig-tested at Abingdon before being fitted.

The almost-complete car was then lowered to the ground floor with a one-ton crane and pushed along the line to be finished.

The ZA had an unusual 'alligator' bonnet opening and made widespread use of walnut inside, particularly on the fascia; another assembly which went on to a jig before being fitted.

The Magnette quickly gained a reputation as a well-made and comfortable sporting saloon and was notably successful in rallying.

Production at Abingdon built up from 8 cars in 1953 to nearly 9000 in 1955 and a total of 18,076 units were made before the ZA was replaced by an even better version, the ZB, in September 1956, which stayed in production until December 1958. Power output went up to 68.4 bhp through fitting larger carburettors, stronger valve springs and increasing the compression ratio from 7.15:1 to 8.3:1.

The Varitone was a further version offered, with two-tone paintwork and a wrap-around rear window, the window itself being made at Morris Motors at Cowley. Some models were sold with Manumatic two-pedal control, a BMC fad that didn't last.

Alas, it was the last of the big MG saloons with some sporting heritage and a link with Abingdon. Some 18,500 ZBs were made before the model was replaced by the BMC Farina line; the name Magnette remained but as a Cowley-built, poorly-disguised version of the Austin Cambridge/Morris Oxford.

Right: ZA Magnettes and export MGAs being built on adjoining lines in the mid-fifties. The ZA can be identified by its 'hockey-stick' trim on the front wing, which was dropped for the ZB. On the line to the left of the Magnettes are Riley Pathfinders, some 5000 of which were built at Abingdon.

Twin-cam troubles

Not everything that MG did was an unalloyed success and one of the two least fortunate episodes of the post-war era was the creation of the MGA twin-cam in 1958. The reasons for its failure are complex; it could have been an outstanding car but it was fundamentally flawed.

There had been some criticism of the standard MGA because of its weight, and John Thornley and Sydney Enever decided to press the BMC management to allow them to build a high-performance competition version. There were reports of a special body being built for it at Coventry, but this was never used.

MG already had a twin-cam engine at its disposal, since Gerald Palmer, deviser of the Magnette, Riley Pathfinder and Jowett Javelin, had designed one at Cowley in 1954. It had run in various MG race and record cars with some success; a version with a Shorrock supercharger had reached 245mph on the Utah salt flats in August 1957 and was to reach 254mph in 1959.

But there was also another contender - a brand-new twin-cam designed by William Appleby at Austin - and the deciding factor was the cost; the Austin engine would have to be productionised, while the Morris version used the bottom end of the B-series engine which was produced at Longbridge. Appleby, perhaps with some justification, was said to be bitter at the decision and maintained that his engine would not have had the problems that were to dog the Morris version, though it seems it was not nearly as powerful.

Mystery surrounds the fate of the twin-cam Austin engine; the lore at Abingdon was that a fitter was called out in the middle of the night to remove it from a car which was about to be shipped to Ireland to run in the TT at Dundrod. The engine was crated up and never seen again, but is believed to have

The prototype MGA twin-cam photographed at the factory. The centre-lock disc wheels were one of the very few styling points that distinguished it from the pushrod version. The twin-cam badges, behind the engine vents on top of the wings, have not yet been fitted.

ended up in a basement at the Motor Industry Research facility.

Meanwhile, there was still a lot of work to do on the Morris twin-cam before it could be put into a road car. The final designs were done by Eddie Maher and Jimmy Thomson at the Morris engine works in Coventry - by coincidence in the buildings that produced the Hotchkiss ohv engine which powered the first MG - Old Number One. And MG had plenty of experience with single overhead cams, as all sports cars between 1929 and 1936 were fitted with them.

Though the block was the standard B, it was bored out to 1588cc to take

Above: The twin-cam engine was a very tight squeeze in the MGA's narrow engine bay. When the MGB was designed its engine bay was made much wider to accommodate various types of engine.

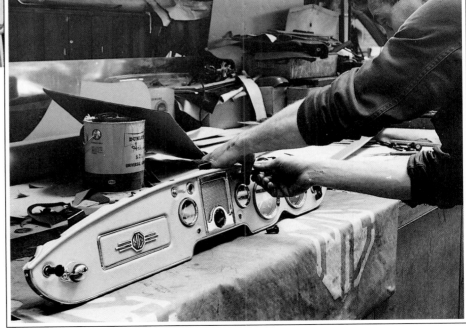

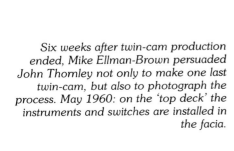

Six weeks after twin-cam production ended, Mike Ellman-Brown persuaded John Thornley not only to make one last twin-cam, but also to photograph the process. May 1960: on the 'top deck' the instruments and switches are installed in the facia.

advantage of the current 1600cc class in international events. Consequently, it had to be finished on a special line, as not only were the bores widened by 2.87 inches but the main bearings were narrower to allow for thicker crank cheeks. They were also heavier duty than the standard copper and lead with steel backings.

The head, of course, was completely new; an aluminum casting at the front of the engine concealed the gears and duplex chains which drove the camshafts. The B block still contained the camshaft housing which was used for the pushrod version, and in this ran a dummy shaft which drove the rev counter. Many of the engine ancillaries had to be moved to allow the engine to squeeze into the MGA's narrow com-

Below: Bolting the dash in position. Note the twin-cam badge to the right of the engine vent.

partment - and this was to lead to trouble later.

Other changes were also necessary: the steering rack had to be moved forward an inch and longer steering arms employed. To carry the extra weight there were suspension changes at the front; revised spring rates and stronger dampers.

One of the twin-cam's problems was access to the distributor. Here, the cap is perched on the fan; the distributor body to the right was concealed beneath the cambox when the body was in place. The car behind is a standard pushrod.

The twin-cam differed from the standard model in engine, brakes and wheels, but assembly procedures were identical. Here, adhesive is applied to the chassis rails as the carpets are put in.

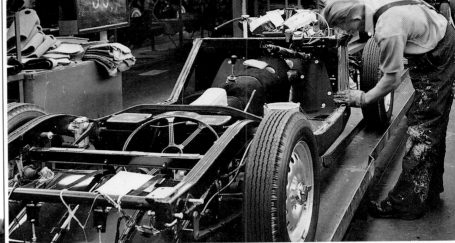

Below: The body descends to the ground floor to be united with chassis number YD1/2611.

Making MGs

Left: Mating chassis and body.

Right: Grille and bumpers have been bolted on as the car nears the end of the line.

Below: Connecting wiring and braking systems.

The gearbox was the same as for the standard MGA, but there was a major departure in the braking system - Dunlop discs were fitted front and rear, like the Jaguars of the time, and there were centre-lock disc wheels similar to those on the D-type. Wire wheels were not offered as an option; Enever disliked them, believing them to be an anachronism although, of course, they were offered on the MGB that followed ...

The prototype began proving runs and problems soon became apparent. Firstly, it overheated because of steam pockets in the head; this was cured by tapping the centre core plug and running a pipe to the header tank. Much more serious was the holing of the pistons. One of the testers at the MIRA track remembers undoing a spark plug and seeing the sun shine on the top of the con rod because the piston crown had disappeared. Work with Champion finding the correct plug alleviated this piston-holing to some extent, but the basic problem was the high compression ratio of 9.9:1.

The domed pistons had chrome rings and the bores themselves were treated with chrome molybdenum, which led to a high oil consumption of one pint every 120 miles. In addition, the piston clearances on the first models were 9 thou, resulting in noisy running. These were later reduced to 4 thou.

Production was planned at 75 a week but this figure was rarely attained. It was obvious from the start that difficulties had not been overcome in the pre-production stage.

The engine was highly-strung, needing careful attention to ignition timing and fuel mixture. To run properly it required high octane petrol, but 83% of the cars were exported to countries where such fuel was not available. In the all-important American market, drivers were not used to tinkering with ignition settings and the distributor was in a most difficult place to reach, which was unfortunate since the points needed adjustment every 3000 miles!

Hurried changes were made after a few weeks: new pistons were used which allowed a lower compression ratio of 8.3:1, reducing power, but improving reliability; revised front springs and shock absorbers were introduced, as the early

versions had worn out quickly leading to poor cornering and scuttle shake. Some time later, to improve access to the buried engine ancillaries, detachable panels were built into the inner wheelarches.

The twin-cam was a fast car - top speed was 114mph compared with 100mph or so for the 1588cc MGA, though 0-60 speed was only 0.4 seconds quicker at 13.3 seconds.

There are those who maintain that the cause of the twin-cam's failure was not the engine itself, but the heavy right foot of insensitive drivers; whatever the reason, the car was withdrawn in 1960, largely because its reputation was damaging MG in the United States. However, of the 2111 made, more than half did

go to America.

Abingdon was left with parts - like wheels and brakes - specific to the twin-cam. These were used up during June and July 1960 on an uncatalogued pushrod model called the De Luxe, which also had the steering and suspension modifications.

One little-known effect of the twin-cam's introduction was that the bonnet line had a larger curvature to clear the top of the cam covers, and all subsequent pushrod MGAs had that bonnet.

It wasn't just the reliability factor that did for the twin-cam, but also increasing competition from other fast sports cars. The irony is that, after being reviled for years, the twin-cam in either roadster or coupe form is now much more sought-after than any other MGA. Indeed, the prototype, ORX 885, was sold at auction in 1995 for well over £20,000,

A final polish in the despatch department for the last twin-cam.

nearly double the value of a pushrod   MGA at the time of its production.

Developing the breed

By the late Fifties, MG had become the world's largest producer of sports cars and, in 1962, the 100,000th MGA was shipped to the United States aboard the *Queen Mary*. It was a special edition in gold with cream trim and whitewall tyres, which was exhibited at the New York motor show before a tour across the country.

Development work went on almost to the end of the MGA's life. During one of the fuel shortages, a smaller, lighter version codenamed EX195 was built with a single carburettor engine and an Austin A30 steering box. There was also research done on smaller engines, including the running of a 1500cc engine on three cylinders, but none of these projects reached fruition.

By 1959, there had also been several experiments to face-lift the car. Changes were made to the back and to the front, but these made the car less aerodynamic and none of them looked quite right, according to those who saw them. This was a tribute to the original design, but other sports cars were now beginning to leave it behind in performance and, in the summer, the new 1600 was launched.

The body, apart from lights and side-screen, was identical to the original MGA, but to make it faster the engine was

The B-series engine and gearbox, which shows the special MGA gearchange casting bolted to the top of the gearbox tailshaft housing. Other versions of BMC cars did not have this casting. This 1600 Mark II block has been liberally treated with engine lacquer!

The 1600 engine in chassis 102392. It's obvious how tight the space was, particularly on the carburettor side of the engine. The installation looks tidier than usual since no screenwashers or heater are fitted. Heaters did not become standard on MG sports cars until 1968.

bored out to 1588cc - the same size as the twin-cam - and Lockheed disc brakes were fitted at the front. Power went up from 68bhp to 80bhp and sales went up with it. The MGA was now a true 100mph sports car.

The new engine size did not last long for, after the demise of the twin-cam, the Austin works at Longbridge had to make a special B-series block just for the new MG, as none of the other BMC cars used the same bore dimensions. This did not make economic sense for a group bent on commonising as many components as possible. So when, in 1961, BMC decided to increase the capacity of its B-series by boring it out to 1622cc, the MGA 1600 MkII, launched in the summer, was the first car to receive the larger engine. The larger capacity increased power still further to 93bhp. In addition, the 1600 MkII had the rear axle ratios from the twin-cam. This was the last change for the MGA as planning of its replacement, the MGB, was already well underway.

In March 1962, the 100,000th MGA came off the line and, after just a few more cars, production came to an end in June, bringing the total to 101,081 cars, the majority of which were exported. It was a notable achievement but an even greater one was to come with the MGB.

In March 1962, while the MGB was being readied for production, the 100,000 MGA came off the line. It went to the United States aboard the Queen Mary to be shown at the New York motor show.

Rebirth of the Midget

The introduction of the MGA in 1955 left MG without a small sports car in the mould of the Midget, which had been so successful in the 1930s and 40s until the TF outstayed its welcome in the mid-50s.

In the federal BMC, the role of the Midget was played by the Austin-Healey Sprite, introduced in 1958 after Donald Healey had been charged to build a small, cheap sports car from existing BMC bits. He took the steering from the

Morris Minor and almost everything else from the Austin A35 - floorpan, 948cc engine, back axle, front suspension and gearbox, though this was improved with closer ratios by the Abingdon competitions department. The new model was

Midget shells were delivered to the top deck with bonnets in place. These were removed at the start of the build process and put back at the end of the line. On this line the cars were pushed backwards.

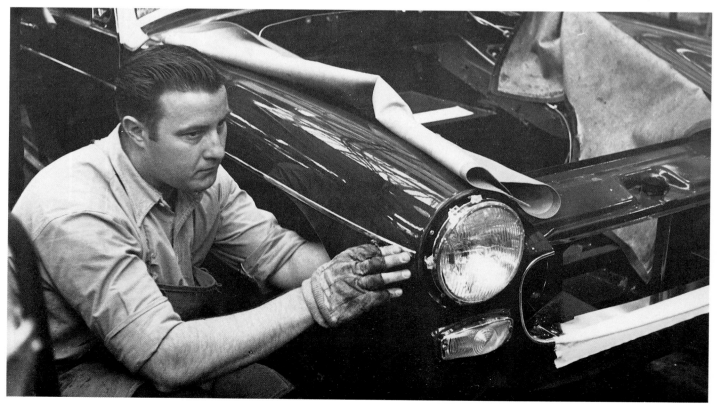

Left, top: Windscreen fitting was one of the first jobs after lights and master cylinder installation.

Left, bottom: Chrome side-trim was fixed on to clips along the flanks.

to have been called the Imp, but Hillman got there first; the name Sprite was bought from Daimler and, with its frogeye headlamps, the new car became one of the most easily-recognised cars on the road.

Though MG had no love for the Austin part of the empire after the MGA prototype was rejected in 1952 in favour of the big Healey, the Sprite was an Abingdon product, built alongside the MGA and Magnette, and it became inevitable that there would be an MG version of it, since badge-engineering was a virus running out of control at BMC.

In May 1961, the bug-eye look disappeared with the introduction of the Sprite Mk II and the Midget arrived a month later. The bug-eye one-piece bonnet had to go, endearing though it was, because it was so vulnerable and expensive to replace. The Healey team redesigned the front of the car, while Sydney Enever and his Abingdon drawing office replaced the back - the early version had no outside access to the boot and was a cause of some irritation to owners trying to stow luggage.

The two cars were identical, other than the radiator grille, badging and minor trim items, though the MG was a few pounds more expensive for no apparent reason.

A line of rubber bumper Midgets on the top deck. Stored on the right, ready for use, are trim panels and steering racks.

Making MGs

Left: Bodyshells start their journey down the line.

Sprites and Midgets were built in a different way to the chassis-based MGA, since their body/chassis was one monocoque unit, built by Pressed Steel at the Swindon works. The bodies were transported firstly to Cowley where they were painted, then delivered by Midlands BRS to the first floor at Abingdon for trimming.

On the ground floor, the front and rear axle assemblies - which, unlike the MGA, were not bolted to a chassis - were put on small four-wheel trolleys running on tracks at shoulder height. The body was then lowered from above, the suspension units bolted on, the A-series engine dropped in and the whole assembly lifted off the trolleys and lowered to the final assembly line. Again, every car was taken out for road testing before despatch.

More than 16,000 Midgets were built with the 998cc engine. In 1962 came the uprated 1093cc engine which also powered the new Austin and Morris 1100 cars. Output went up from 46 to 55bhp;

The A-series engine is dropped in while the front disc brakes are checked. Just below the disc unit can be seen one of the wheels of the trolley on which the bodies were moved until they gained their own wheels.

disc brakes were standardised on the front wheels and a larger clutch was fitted. In March 1964, the interior was upgraded, with wind-up windows instead of side-screens, a curved windscreen and lockable exterior door handles. More importantly, the rear suspension was revised; the original car had little lateral location of the rear axle and a tendency to oversteer, which the adoption of half-elliptic springs did much to cure. Power was boosted again in 1966

for the Mark III, which used a detuned version of the Mini-Cooper1275cc unit, giving 65bhp.

Over the next few years there were cosmetic changes, not all of them happy, particularly the 1969 revamp in British Leyland Black. In 1971 the Austin-Healey Sprite version disappeared when the licence to use the Healey name ran out, though there was an *Austin* Sprite until July of that year. Nearly 130,000 Sprites were made, a figure easily surpassed by the Midget, which continued in production for another eight years.

In 1974 came the adoption of the Triumph Spitfire 1493cc engine, made at the Radford plant in Coventry, which was mated with the gearbox from the Morris Marina. The reason for its adoption was that it was not worth de-toxing the Midget's engine for the US. The '1500' produced the same output - 65bhp at 5500rpm - rather less than it did in the Spitfire because of different

33

Making MGs

The wheels are on and a twist of the wrist tightens the centre-lock wires.

Right: The air cleaner is screwed on.

The rolling chassis descends from the elevated line for final components to be fitted.

Making MGs

The chrome grille with MG octagon is bolted in place.

Final inspection for a very early Mark I Midget bound for the US.

36

manifolding arrangements, and for American use was, like the MGB, eventually fitted with a single Stromberg carburettor instead of two SUs. It also acquired its own version of the 'rubber' bumpers - in fact, made of polyurethane. Although hammered by the motoring press, the alterations did not seem to affect sales, which ran at an average of

Midgets and Sprites being assembled on adjoining lines. It was here that bumpers were affixed and the bonnet refitted. Between the lines can be seen stocks of bumpers and hood frames. To the left of the picture is the MGA line, and beyond that again a line producing Morris Minor vans. (Courtesy BMIHT/Rover Group)

*Left: The same line as shown in the
previous photograph at a much later date,
with export Midgets moving towards
engine installation. (Courtesy BMIHT/
Rover Group)*

around 14,000 a year through the Seventies until production stopped in December 1979 after a total of 224,817 cars.

The last car went down the line on December 7 with a note taped to the

*The 1493cc Triumph engine from the Spitfire replaced the A-series unit in 1974. Carburettors were on the opposite side.
(Courtesy BMIHT/Rover Group)*

Making MGs

The last delivery to Abingdon of Midget bodies. On the top car is a mock wreath with a union jack flag.

Below: The last Midget comes down the line in December 1979, with a "Save Abingdon" sticker on the window.

windscreen "Gone but not forgotten." It was destined for Japan, a curious irony since the British Leyland masterplan for Abingdon at that time was to end all car production there within a year and use the works to stock imported Japanese parts for a Honda clone, the Triumph Acclaim, which was to be to be built at Cowley.

Final inspection for the last Midget. The final 500 cars were all black. The sticker on the right of the windscreen says: "Gone but not forgotten."

MGß - the world bestseller

A very early MGB tourer bound for the US, photographed before the car had even been announced.

The world's bestselling sports car arrived in 1962 and more than half a million were produced before Abingdon closed for good in 1980.

The MGA was still selling strongly when design studies for its replacement were begun and it became obvious that the separate chassis had had its day. Unitary construction meant economies of production and BMC's huge new Pressed Steel plant at Stratton St Margaret, Swindon, was well able to cope with demand.

Many styling exercises were done, one of which was from the Italian studios of Frua, who rebodied an MGA with a rather florid coupe body. When it was rejected, it was cut up at Abingdon in front of the local customs official to avoid import duty. But the shape which finally defined the MGB was the work of Don Hayter, the chief body draughtsman, who had previously worked for Aston Martin. In this classic shape, which survived for so many years, some saw Aston influences, others Ferrari and there were even those who detected a touch of the Renault Caravelle.

A roadster prototype was ready by 1960, albeit with experimental coil spring suspension at the rear, which did not survive, as leaves proved simpler and cheaper. Two more prototypes were made, one with many aluminium panels, as in the MGA, though, in the production cars, these were steel with the exception of the bonnet. Testing went on at Chalgrove airfield nearby which identified a scuttle shake problem, which led to the fascia being reinforced.

Much of the engineering was carried over from the MGA. The MGB shared

The monocoque body/chassis unit of the MGB was extremely strong and the double bulkhead gave great rigidity. This picture was taken in 1962: compare it with those in Chapter 12. (Courtesy BMIHT/Rover Group)

Making MGs

44

Seventeen years later, the procedure is the same: piles of rear leaf springs (right) wait for fitting, followed by the front suspension assemblies (centre right).

the B-series engine and gearbox, though there had been several studies done on fitting different engines, among them the Daimler V8 and a new BMC 2-litre Vee engine, which never went into volume production because of vibration problems, though two or three cars were fit- ted with it. Indeed, because of the possibility of fitting a Vee engine, the engine compartment was made much wider than was necessary for the in-line four, which was to prove of benefit when the Rover V8 engine came along.

Had the car inherited the B-series engine from the MGA with its capacity at 1622cc (which was the original plan) there would have been a problem as the new car was some 50lbs heavier and would have incurred a performance penalty. But the faithful B was bored out to 1789cc, not especially for the MG but

After axle fitment, exhaust systems and wheels were fitted before the rolling 'chassis' was craned down to ground level.

John Thornley poses with the new MGB GT in May 1966; the publicity department claimed that such was the demand for the car, he was unable to have one himself. In the background is the administration building, with his office on the first floor. The building still survives.

for the forthcoming BMC 1800 saloon. The wider under-bonnet area allowed the use of Coopers canister-type air filters with paper elements, which were said to improve breathing substantially.

The bored-out power plant gave 95bhp at 5400rpm, compared with 93bhp for the smaller engine, and there was an increase in torque from 97lbft at 4000rpm to 110lbft at 3000rpm. Maximum speed in the last MGA was 101mph with a 0-60mph figure of 13.3 seconds; the B gave 103mph and took 12.2 seconds.

The method of manufacture changed little from that of the MGA, other than that there was no chassis on which to assemble the running gear. But the hull of the car was extremely strong as the floorpan was braced with three substantial longitudinal members.

The body panels were stamped out at Swindon and went next to Morris Bodies at Coventry, where the panels were welded together and the completed shell dipped in primer and spray painted. They took this route until the Coventry factory closed in 1971 when assembly moved to Cowley. Then, in double-deck transporters, they arrived at Abingdon's 'top deck' for trimming and installation of Lucas electrics.

On the floor beneath the top deck, the track was not almost at ground level, as with the MGA line, but at shoulder height or above, as was the practice with the monocoque Midget.

Components were, in almost all cases, from the same suppliers as those for the MGA. The big mechanical units came from the same Birmingham BMC factories at Longbridge and Ward End.

John Thompson, who had supplied the MGA's chassis parts from Wolverhampton, provided the front crossmember, Cam Gears the steering, Smiths the instruments and the modified A40 heater. Borg and Beck supplied the clutch, Lockheed the brakes and Dunlop the wheels and tyres. Laycock supplied the optional overdrive, locks and overriders came from Wilmot Breeden and the hoods and tonneau covers from Coventry Hood and Seating. It's notable that, as far as one can gather, all the components were sourced from British companies, most of them in the Midlands. How very different from today's form of manufacture, when parts may come from any-

where in the world.

The first production cars were built in May 1962, while MGA output was tailing off. The MGB was due for launch in September, just before the London motor show, by which time some 700 cars had been built, most of them for export.

The MGB was an immediate and justified success and its lines were so right from the very start that few changes were needed in its 18-year life, other than those which were cosmetic or forced by American legislation. The cars began to pour off the lines at Abingdon - 23,000 in 1963, 26,000 the next year. Production never fell below 23,000 until the year

The GT made clever use of space, though the 'occasional' rear seat offered almost no legroom. The sectioned car (below), which is in the Heritage Motor Centre at Gaydon, is believed to have been prepared for the Turin motor show in 1967.

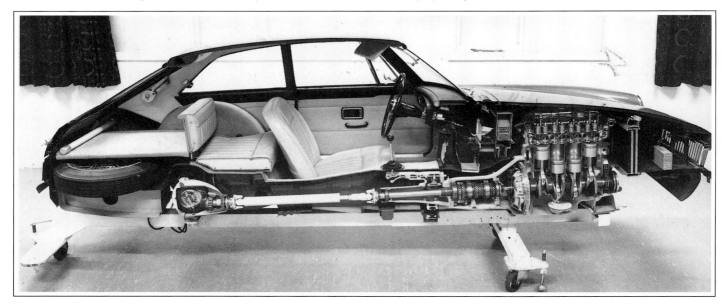

the factory closed; in 1972 it was approaching 40,000 - with the Midget, 55,000 - an outstanding achievement.

The other notable achievement was the vast number exported; every year, between 75 and 80% of roadsters went abroad.

The first mechanical change came at the end of 1964, when the B-series engine was given five main bearings instead of three, as it was to power the new BMC

1800 range. Five bearings gave a stronger bottom end, but the additional frictional losses caused the engine to rev less freely. At the same time the oil cooler, initially an optional extra, was made standard.

The major MG event of the following year was the introduction of the GT - which had been long in the planning - John Thornley's 'poor man's Aston Martin'. It was styled at Abingdon but the

final detailing was done by Pininfarina, who built the first prototype. Unlike the roadster, the body was completed at Pressed Steel at Swindon, then finished with paint and trim at Cowley.

While the MGA coupe was a hardtop welded to the roadster body, the line of the GT was far more subtle, with a higher windscreen than the MGB roadster and a sloping tail. There were changes beneath the skin; the floorpan

The engine of the first production MGBGT, a works car registered ERX 498C, was used extensively for publicity shots. This picture was taken before the car was actually used and the rocker cover still has 'coupe' written on it in chalk. (Courtesy BMIHT/Rover Group)

was different to allow for the vestigial seating at the rear. A heavier duty and quieter-running Salisbury rear axle was fitted, which was later used for the tourer also.

Again, there was acclaim for another great Abingdon product which, although some 160lbs heavier than the tourer, was only slightly slower and could still top the magic 100mph. Demand for the GT was so great that BMC stopped employees buying it through the staff purchase

49

Early MGBs were available with leather seats but, by 1972, plastic had taken over and the Hyde group of ICI made almost all this interior trim. Seat facings were in Ambla vinyl-coated fabric, with breathing Amblair inserts. Seat backs were in pvc-coated Vynide, which was also used in double-coated form for the hood. Door panels were in Novon and the crash panels formed from Vulkide shock absorbent ABS sheet.

scheme, and much was made by the publicity department of the fact that John Thornley himself was not allowed to have one. Production rates, however, ran much lower than those of the tourer, and there was not the same push for exports; in fact, more cars were sold on the home market than went abroad.

In 1967 came the Mk II versions of the MGB roadster and GT, with all-synchromesh gearbox, new to the BMC range which required changes to the

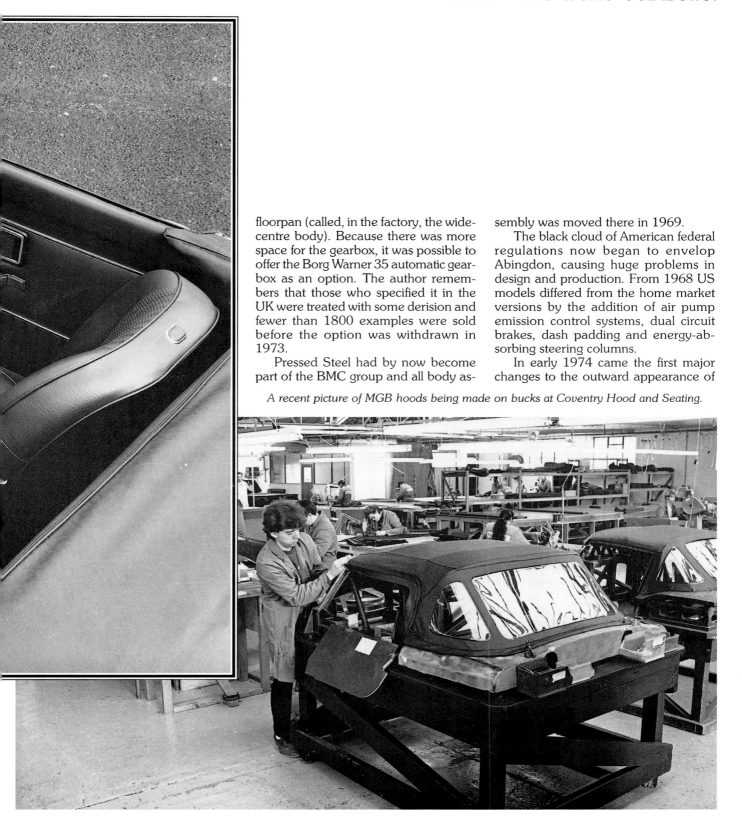

floorpan (called, in the factory, the wide-centre body). Because there was more space for the gearbox, it was possible to offer the Borg Warner 35 automatic gearbox as an option. The author remembers that those who specified it in the UK were treated with some derision and fewer than 1800 examples were sold before the option was withdrawn in 1973.

Pressed Steel had by now become part of the BMC group and all body as-sembly was moved there in 1969.

The black cloud of American federal regulations now began to envelop Abingdon, causing huge problems in design and production. From 1968 US models differed from the home market versions by the addition of air pump emission control systems, dual circuit brakes, dash padding and energy-ab-sorbing steering columns.

In early 1974 came the first major changes to the outward appearance of

A recent picture of MGB hoods being made on bucks at Coventry Hood and Seating.

Making MGs

On the top deck, where trim and wiring were done, shells were pushed around the wooden floor on small trolleys, guided by a metal channel.

the cars. For the American market huge rubber overriders were fitted front and rear, which became known as 'Mae Wests' or 'Sabrinas' (a bosomy British starlet). These did not last long for, in September, appeared the controversial so-called 'rubber bumpers', required to meet US legislation. The first ones tried were, in fact, made of rubber, but it was found that polyurethane was a better absorbent. Implementation of the new bumpers was delayed by tooling problems at Vitafoam in Manchester. California state regulations had now decreed

Right: Lucas light units are screwed into a line of GTs.

that a 5mph impact should cause no damage at all to the car. The only alternative to polyurethane bumpers was moving bumpers with energy absorbers behind, but this would have made the car substantially longer than the five inches that the new bumpers added.

Behind the bumpers, at the back and front of the car, were large steel beams

The engine is shoe-horned into the shell on the ground floor. (Courtesy BMIHT/Rover Group)

Left: At the next stage, connections between car and engine are made. From 1975, US models like this were fitted with a single Stromberg carburettor, which reduced power substantially. (Courtesy BMIHT/Rover Group)

Right: The device in the centre, on to which the car is about to be rolled, is a Weaver machine, used for adjusting tracking.

which added a not inconsiderable 80 or so pounds in weight. In addition, the ride height of the car had to be increased to conform with the US regulation that bumpers should be between 16 and 20 inches from the ground, front and rear. Altering the rear sringing points and the front crossmember added 1.5 inches to the ride height of the car, making handling less precise, though a rear anti-roll bar was fitted later to ameliorate the wallowing.

Outrage followed when the same bumpers appeared - unnecessarily, it seemed - on home market models. But, because so much of MG production went to America, it was not economically viable to retain the chrome bumpers since there had been a major change in the frontal structure of the car to accommodate the alterations necessary for the US market. Happily, the home market did not suffer the same fate the following year, when the twin SU carburettors were replaced on US models with a single Stromberg CD, a special cylinder head with smaller valves and a catalytic converter.

MG workers christened this US ver-

Final inspection at the end of the MGB line. Bonnets - stored on the left - were one of the last components to be installed.

Left, top: The paintshop in B block where rectification was done. Note the masking.

Left, bottom: Hundreds of export models in the compound wait to be taken to the docks. The large side-flashers were not seen on home market models.

In January 1980 the half-millionth MGB was made. The black roadster was one of a limited edition with a motif on the side marking 50 years of production at Abingdon, and was destined for the United States. On the right is Sydney Enever and on the left Alan Edis, who was supposed to have been in charge of export packing at Abingdon when MG production finished later that year, but this did not happen.

sion 'the gutless wonder', for output was down by about 20bhp and the car not much faster than the TD of the fifties. It took 18.3 seconds to reach 60mph and had a top speed of 90mph, compared with the home market version's 12.2 seconds and 103mph.

However, the car continued to sell well in its new guise and it can be argued that, if one lived in smog-shrouded Los Angeles, with its 50mph speed limit, emission controls were a very good thing and performance not so important.

MGC - the great unloved

The quest to put an even more powerful engine into the MGB had begun even before the car was launched. There were drawings for a six-cylinder version dating from 1961, but nothing happened for several years until BMC started casting around for a replacement for the Austin-Healey 3000.

Introduced in 1954, the big Healey

The large and very heavy six-cylinder engine of the MGC. On early versions like this, rocker covers were painted with a black crackle finish, which got very dirty. The finish was later changed to light green. Note the huge oil filter.

was assembled first at Longbridge and then, from 1957, at Abingdon. Not only was it long in the tooth, it shared little with other BMC products and the relationship with Jensen, who built the shells, was not happy.

So in the new world of badge-engineering it seemed logical to have a six-cylinder car using common BMC parts and the MGB shell with one Healey and one MG version. After all, the Midget and the Sprite built on parallel production lines at Abingdon were virtually identical and both of those sold well. Consequently, design studies were begun with the code name ADO 52 for the MG and ADO 51 for the Healey and a prototype chassis existed in 1964. Don Hayter, chief draughtsman at the time, was asked to put a Healey grille on the latter version. This was not to Donald Healey's taste and he continued with the development of a new big Healey with the 4-litre Rolls-Royce engine from the Vanden Plas Princess R; this plan came to nothing as BMC would not support it.

For the new MG, the logical solution would have been to put the Healey's 2912cc truck-like engine into the MGB shell, but it was too big to squeeze in and far too heavy. Since, at that time, BMC had something of an overseas presence, other parts of the empire were scoured for an engine.

In Australia, the 'Blue Flash' six of 2433cc was being made which was essentially the B-series 1622cc engine with two extra cylinders. One was installed in a brown GT for assessment but gave little extra performance and would have to have been imported from the other side of the world, even though the crank-

shaft was made at Longbridge. Daimler's V8 engine and the Jaguar XK unit were also considered.

However, BMC itself was at work in Coventry on a new six-cylinder engine, which would power the Austin 3-litre, one of the ugliest and least-successful cars ever made by a volume manufacturer. The brief on which the engines department was working was to make the old six-cylinder smoother, lighter and smaller; advances in casting techniques would allow thinner cylinder walls.

There was dismay at Abingdon, however, when the results appeared. The new unit, still 2912cc, was only 1.75ins shorter than the engine it replaced and was too tall to fit under the bonnet without modification. But, more importantly, instead of saving the promised 90lbs in weight, the designers had saved only 20lbs. In addition, performance was cut by poor porting in the cylinder head and seven main bearings, which led to high frictional losses. It was memorably described in the *Autocar* by Michael Scarlett who said "it appears to have been drawn up by an ex-marine diesel engineer who was transferred against his will to the tractor engine department."

Installed in the MGB, the 150bhp engine - half as powerful again as the B - made the car look as if it were on its knees. John Thornley said later that if the engine had been anywhere near right, it would have been a sensation: "as it was we had to make a botched-up job of the front suspension; if we had known the engine would be 70lbs overweight we would have designed a different suspension". As it was, the entire front of the MGB chassis frame had to

be redesigned to accommodate the bigger engine and, for a time, it looked as if de Dion suspension - considered for the MGA - would be used at the rear, but this was abandoned because of cost and complexity, and the MGB's semi-elliptic springs and live rear axle were retained.

Underneath, the front was quite different. To make room for the bigger engine, Pat Rees in the design office at Cowley, designed a tubular crossmember to replace the substantial metal item in the MGB. Instead of coil springs there were telescopic dampers, with long torsion bars transferring the loads from the front wishbones to securing points under the seats. It was the system fitted to the Minor and one which was used extensively in the old Morris empire. The front of the floorpan and the inner wings were a different shape to those of the MGB.

This suspension set-up was designed for the promised lighter engine, so hurried adjustments had to be made when the new engine arrived. There were minor revisions to the panelwork, too; because the engine was so long, the radiator was moved forward and a step had to be put in the bonnet to clear it. There was also a bulge in the bonnet to accommodate the front carburettor.

The MGC did not look significantly different to the standard MGB, which was part of the marketing problem, but the Abingdon men had only a small budget at their disposal and large metalwork changes were out of the question. In 1967, the first MGCs came off the production line and into a torrent of abuse. Lack of torque and chronic understeer were alleged.

There were hurt feelings at Abingdon; the apologists claimed the reason the car seemed to corner badly was, as the engine was so quiet, people used to MGBs were attempting to corner too quickly. Of the ruffled feathers, Mike Allison, who worked for BMC at the time, says: "Before production we [Quality] tested cars on the road and at Silverstone and found the cars driveable and as fast as Bill Nicholson's Racing MGB on the circuit. It was only the journalists who complained - and, at the time, they rubbished anything BMC tried to do. We [BMC] had had umpteen years with ADO16 (1100) the bestseller, and now it was Ford's turn with the relatively inferior Cortina!"

The 19-year-old Prince of Wales bought an MGC GT after a test drive at Buckingham Palace. It was delivered to his college at Cambridge with one strange extra fitted by the factory - an extra-loud bull-horn for calling cattle. However, the royal purchase did not encourage a rush to the showrooms ...

In 1968, when about 100 MGCs a week were being produced (compared with 500 MGBs), the rear axle ratio was revised to give better acceleration. There were also some experiments with fuel injection, but nothing could be done about the nose-heavy characteristics of the car, for the weight distribution was 55.7% at the front and 44.3% at the rear, compared to 52.5% front and 47.5% rear for the B.

However, in a straight line it was an excellent tourer and could be very fast. MG test driver, Tommy Haig-, a scion of the whisky family, took one up to 140mph with overdrive engaged on the autobahn in Germany

Of the 9000 produced - almost equally divided between tourer and GT versions - the US took half. Drivers there had even more to complain about since Federal emission regulations strangled the output, reducing it to roughly the same as the MGB. Also, two servos were fitted for the dual braking system; because they took up so much space, engine temperatures rose and fans had to be fitted to cool the carburettors.

The substantial changes needed to accommodate the six-cylinder engine can be seen by comparing the MGC underside with the standard MGB. In the MGB (above) the front of the engine lies well behind the steering rack and anti-roll bar; in the MGC (right) the rack is underneath the sump. The torsion bars running longitudinally can be clearly seen.

Production came to an ignominious end in September 1969 after two years. As with the twin-cam, there were bodies and engines left on the battlefield. Some, almost all GTs, were bought by the London distributor University Motors, who modified the engines and sold the cars successfully. Earlier, to try and boost the car, the competitions department had six special shells made by Pressed Steel. These retained the steel floorpan but had light alloy body panels and heavily-modified engines. One finished 10th at Sebring in 1968 and the following year another reached 15th place. It was all too late, but didn't stop Abingdon making one last attempt to make a bigger, faster MGB.

Testing, testing ...

One of the traditions at MG was to road test each new car for several miles. The routes changed over the years but, from the late Forties, the pattern was to drive out of the gate to Sheepstead crossroads to the west of Abingdon and return by the same route. Using different road surfaces, various problems could be isolated, and when the cars returned to the factory those in need of improvement went to the rectification department.

Brian Moylan, who worked there for a while, recalled that most of the mechanical problems were caused by loose-fitting bonnets, suspension rattles and faulty components such as noisy gearboxes and rear axles. Some cars went out on test again, the driver accompanied by a fitter or inspector.

Routine road testing stopped in 1975 when a roller dynamometer was installed. There was one exception, the MGBGT V8, which had always been tested on a much longer route, including a fast section of the A420.

A quality engineering department was set up in the Sixties in order to monitor persistent defects and to liaise with suppliers about component faults.

Before the American safety regulations caused havoc at Abingdon, rudimentary crash testing was also done at the works, as the chrome bumper cars

MGAs and a ZA Magnette setting out from the Marcham Road gate for the six-mile road test. In the background is a Riley Pathfinder, which was also assembled at Abingdon. The door on the right led to the despatch department. (Courtesy BMIHT/ Rover Group)

were designed to withstand a 5mph impact with relatively little damage. The tests were done on a seven foot high ramp angled at 45 degrees. Inside the car, as it hurtled down into a solid wall at the bottom, sat a hapless member of the experimental shop!

When US legislation demanded higher safety standards, MG built its own test rig at the factory rather than use the motor industry research facilities at Nuneaton, which cost £1000 a time. The MG version was built for £15,000, plus another £2000 for instruments, and, by 1975, 25 cars a year were being crashed to meet safety standards in various parts of the world. The rig worked by harnessing a Jaguar engine to a winch, to which the cars were connected. It hurled them down a track and into the wall at 30mph. The tests showed that the new engineering at the front prevented impact damage to the passenger area, transmitting the shock under the car to the rear. Although the bonnet crumpled, the body damage did not extend beyond the windscreen, and the splintered windscreen did not fall on the passengers.

New US safety legislation had been passed in 1967, largely as a result of the campaign by Ralph Nader and his book *Unsafe at any Speed*. The new rules sought not only to protect the occupants of the car in a crash, through impact-absorbent steering and better padding, but also to make exhaust emissions less toxic. So MG had to build an air pollution centre at the factory in 1967. Excavations for the foundations uncovered a grisly secret: eight skeletons, 1500 years old, lay beneath the surface; one had been beheaded and the head placed on

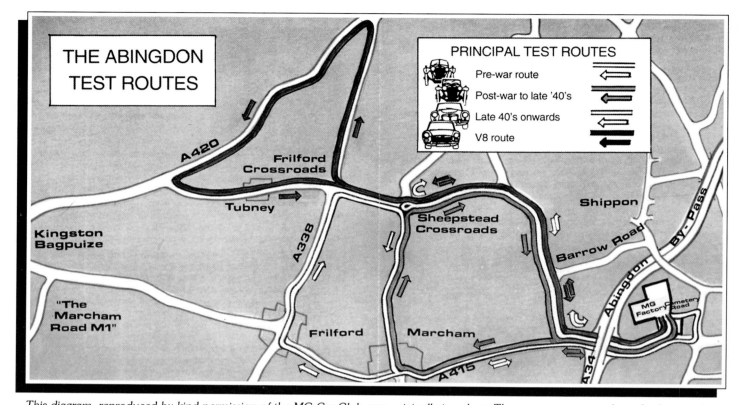

This diagram, reproduced by kind permission of the MG Car Club, was originally in colour. The pre-war route ran from the factory along the A415 to the A338 at Frilford and back down to Marcham; from post-war to the late forties, it ran to Marcham and Sheepstead, completing a circle. From the fifties to the end of road testing, cars ran to the Sheepstead crossroads and back along the same route. The V8 was tested on the longest route, through Sheepstead crossroads to Frilford crossroads and out along the A420.

Left: Wind tunnel testing at Austin. Air was drawn outwards by the giant fan at the back, as is clearly demonstrated by the flying ribbons of the 'fishing rod' that the very cold man is holding! (Courtesy BMIHT/Rover Group)

Right, top: A GT hits the test wall at 30mph with no distortion to the passenger area.

Right, bottom: Crash testing was also carried out on the rear of the car where, again, the shock was absorbed.

The line between the front and rear row of cars was the track of the home-made rig down which the test cars were hurled into the wall.

the chest.

The new unit cost £60,000 and inside the 200ft long building was a 'soak' area, in which up to 15 cars were left at a temperature of 70degrees before being tested on a rolling road. Acceleration and deceleration tests on each car had to be done seven times as the exhaust gases were collected and analysed. Early attempts at trying to reduce emissions by recycling exhaust gases had caused engines to boil, but the problem was overcome.

Mike Allison, who became Chief Quality Engineer, set up and ran the new facility. He says: "It was known as the 'A.P.C.C.' (Air Pollution Control Centre). The test was a standard procedure in which gases were monitored on a continuous basis and results analyseds statistically. European laws and later Californian standards revised procedures in which the gases were analysed on a sam-

ple basis. The A.P.C.C. was the first such production facility in the world".

The time and money spent on making cars meet the new US standards was immense, and affected MG more than any other manufacturer since 65% of all production at that time went to the United States.

An engineering team, under the supervision of Sydney Enever, worked flat out to meet the requirements, and Roy Brocklehurst, then his assistant, made three trips to America to try to make sense of the regulations, which changed frequently. For instance, at one point twin reversing lights were specified which were designed and the tooling made; then the specification was changed to only one light.

The positioning of seat belt anchorages, specified by legislation to be at certain angles based on American cars, would have meant that, in the MGB, one

would have been above the car in the open air! Doorlocks had to be redesigned to withstand 2500lbs of pressure.

A great deal of lobbying went on to try to minimise the effect of the legislation, but, as the car safety issue began to have a worldwide impact in the late Sixties, it was not only America that required a different specification to the UK market cars. California had its own version of the US specification and there were different requirements in Canada, Australia, Japan and many European countries.

All these changes had to designed, engineered, tested and checked on the production lines. The result was that resources were diverted away from major improvements to existing models and serious consideration of any brand-new MG was postponed.

From the mid-Sixties onwards, demands from the US and other countries led to increasingly complex test routines for each car. The picture right shows a 1972 US-specification roadster being tested on the dynamometer. In the picture above a similar car is being run at 30mph at full working temperature. Crash padding on the passenger side was known as the 'Abingdon pillow'.

The V8 cars

Since the MGC's demise, desultory attempts had been made to find a bigger engine for the MGB and two small V8 engines were available in the BL group; the home-grown 2997cc version in the Triumph Stag and the ex-Buick 3528cc bought originally for the big Rovers and supplied to Morgan for its Plus Eight. There had also been some experimentation with the 4561cc V8 from the Daimler Majestic Major.

In the meantime, private enterprise

The Rover V8 engine fitted comfortably into the MGB shell, but the carburettors were resited at the end of the block to avoid a bonnet bulge. The inlet tracts were specially designed for this application. Note the size of the engine steady, which did not appear on production cars.

development of a V8 car went ahead from 1970, as engineer Ken Costello dropped the Rover unit into a standard MGB, marketing the version with great success and attracting plaudits for the car's performance, as acceleration was much improved and the top speed more than 120mph.

The MGB's engine compartment had been designed originally to take a wide engine, as a V8 had been considered at the outset, so it was easy to insert the big alloy engine without major sheet metal changes. The Costello's favourable reception prompted BL management to spur Abingdon into producing a V8 prototype of its own, using the low-compression engine from the Range-Rover, and the car was available within six weeks of the go-ahead being given.

The big advantage of the Rover unit was that it gave a huge increase in power, but, because of its alloy construction, it actually weighed 40lbs *less* than the MGB engine. Although there was a higher compression version of it available, this was not used because it required high octane fuel, which was being phased out.

One difficulty with the Rover unit was that it had far greater torque than the standard B-series engine which, it was considered, the roadster shell, as it was then engineered, could not handle. The MGC shell might have coped, but the tooling had been scrapped in 1969. As a result, the new car was made as a GT only, with the inner wheelarches and front bulkhead reshaped to allow for the larger engine.

Supplies of Rover engines to Costello were cut off as the first production cars were built in 1973. These differed from his version substantially; there was, for instance, a larger clutch, stronger rear springs and special alloy wheels. In addition, the SU carburettors were moved to the rear of the engine, thus avoiding a bulge in the bonnet. Seven or eight versions were produced to US specification and sent to America. These, however, were returned and the car was never sold there - reputedly because of the internal rivalries between BL's sports car divisions of MG, Triumph and Jaguar.

But, fine car though it was, with effortless performance - one version clocked nearly 140mph - it must be con-sidered a commercial failure, through no fault of MG. Even in the home market production was restricted, for there were so many calls on the Rover engine, not only for use in the Range-Rover but also the two other Rover saloons, that insufficient engines were available for Abingdon's needs.

Then the Middle East war began - and the price of oil doubled. Though petrol consumption of the V8 was not significantly higher than that of the MGB, because it had a much bigger engine it was perceived as a gas-guzzler. Graham Robson, in his excellent book *The MGA, MGB and MGC,* identifies yet another reason - it was 48% more expensive than the MGB - a mark-up imposed to protect Triumph's TR6 and Stag.

Most of the V8s were chrome bumpered - 1856, compared with 735 rubber bumpered cars.

The last of the 2591 cars was made in September 1976. It could not have been imagined then that the model would return, in slightly different guise, nearly two decades later.

Working on the line

Abingdon was renowned throughout the various major groups to which it belonged - Nuffield, BMC, British Motor Holdings and British Leyland - for its industrial harmony, though given the strife that raged in the motor industry in the 1960s and 70s this was, in some senses, a comparative judgement.

There was, however, far less union militancy at Abingdon than at nearby Cowley, though sometimes MG would be dragged into disputes. And because the factory was entirely dependent on parts being produced elsewhere, stoppages at Pressed Steel or at Longbridge or Cowley had an immediate effect by bringing MG lines to a standstill within a day or so.

There were small local disputes as well; in February 1970, for instance, after one of the coldest nights of the year, men who handled the body shells coming off the transporters on to the top deck walked out because they said the shells, which were covered in frost and ice, were too cold to handle.

Workers throughout the motor industry were traditionally paid piece-work rates; they were given a daily quota of units to produce and paid by results. They worked in cycles of between seven and ten minutes - that is to say each line task took this amount of time to complete before the next unit arrived.

Brian Moylan recalls that most of the workers on the line were local tradesmen not connected with the motor industry - plumbers, painters and decorators - who worked at MG almost in their spare time. "On the line they worked like hell, because the sooner they could get through their quota and get home, the sooner they could start on their proper jobs". In the days of full production, though, they would work a full day and sometimes overtime as well.

The work was constantly checked by inspectors, who were not paid piece-work rates and were rather envious of those who were, so "they didn't let the lads get away with anything." Piece-work had led to constant disputes throughout the car industry and, in the 70s, it was replaced at British Leyland by a system called measured day work, in which units had to be produced over a standard working day. This led to problems of a different kind. When the TR7 was being produced - at the expense of MGB production (which the men at Abingdon say was deliberately suppressed), the workers could not fill the day. Moylan says: "It got the factory quite a bad name locally, because for quite a lot of the time in the summer you could see men lying about in the sun with their shirts off."

It was not just the Abingdon workers who assembled MGs, for the MGA, MGB and Midget were all assembled overseas from CKD (completely knocked-down) kits sent out in crates from Abingdon. MGAs, for instance, went to Australia, without any trim, tyres and rear springs. For the MGA, the main overseas assemblers were Nuffield Australia in New South Wales, British Car Distributors in Durban, South Africa, Booth Poole, in Dublin, Republic of Ireland, J.J. Molenaar in Amersfoot, Netherlands and Automoviles Ingleses, Mexico City.

Not as many plants were used for the MGB; the great majority of the 10,498 CKD roadsters were put together in Australia, with a few in Dublin and at the BL works at Malines in Belgium. Midgets were not assembled in Australia as the Sprite was marketed there in its place.

All Australian assembly came to a halt when the government declared that cars manufactured there had to have a local content of 85%, which was not feasible for MG production.

There was also a 'semi-knocked-down' version of some cars, which involved many fewer parts being exported. An example was the Midget that was assembled in Milan by Innocenti, which had a body by Ghia. Some 17,500 examples were built.

Life at Abingdon was not all unremitting toil; these elaborate decorations were put up on the final MGB assembly line for Christmas 1976. At the rear can be seen a giant Father Christmas.

How the parts were packed in 'completely knocked-down' form for overseas assembly. There are four MGA chassis and numerous other components on this pallet! (Courtesy BMIHT/Rover Group)

The end of Abingdon

In the late seventies, the need for a new sports car was perceived as urgent, but British Leyland's £70 million investment money went not into MG but the Tri-umph TR7, built at the Speke No 2 plant on Merseyside. It was all to end in a rela-tively unsuccessful car built in a factory whose quality control difficulties became legendary. Production was transferred eventually to Coventry

Among MG men there is some bit-terness that the Abingdon plant was

The last roadster - or not? The one pictured was white, whereas the final documented tourer, in the Heritage Centre at Gaydon, is beige metallic. The confusion may have arisen because the shell arrived from Pressed Steel with bunting attached; it may have been the last shell to be made at Swindon.

Making MGs

starved of much-needed investment; Cecil Cousins, on a visit to the US found that dealers there who had ordered 20 MGBs were getting only 10 of them, plus 10 TR7s they didn't want but had to take. "There was no doubt" says Brian Moylan "that MGB production was being suppressed." Triumph tried hard to make its new investment pay, but the cost was borne at Abingdon.

Development of the MGB was effectively stopped in 1978 and the car never received the version of the 'O' series engine designed for it to overcome the emission problem.

MG's problems were compounded in 1979 by the return to power of the Conservative government when the pound soared against the dollar. Sir Michael Edwardes, chairman of BL at the time, said: "It brought BL to its knees". It was

Above & below: The day the Abingdon workers collected their wages for the last time; desolate scenes in the assembly block. John Thornley, MG's guiding light said: "I was shocked to see the place so empty."

reckoned that MG was losing £900 on every car sold in the States and 80% of

production went there. At one time there were up to 6000 unsold cars in America and production was cut back from 600 cars a week to 380.

It could not go on. In the first week of September 1979 there had been bunting and celebrations to mark 50 years of MG production at Abingdon. The following Monday, September 10 - 'black Monday' as it became known in MG folklore - closure was announced. The outcry was huge; various efforts were made to save the factory, includ-

ing a substantial bid by a consortium headed by Aston Martin, but it was all in vain.

Just over a year later the last two MGBs were finished. Part of the Limited Edition - 1000 cars finished in pewter or bronze metallic paint - the car was described as "... the most loved, famous sports car that has ever been built", according to the publicity.

One of the last tourers went down

the line on October 22 1980, garlanded with flowers and union jack flags, which had been put on at the Swindon Pressed Steel works. The final tourer was a bronze metallic version registered HOK 681W. The very last car was a metallic pewter GT, registration number HOK 682W. They are now both in the Heritage Motor Centre at Gaydon, Warwickshire.

On October 24 that year the work-

24 October 1980, the number 3 gate on the Marcham Road; inactivity for the first time in more than 50 years.

ers came in for the last time to collect final pay packets.

There is some debate about whether it would have been worth saving Abingdon; the site was small by modern standards and facilities antiquated and in need of huge investment. What money BL had in 1979 went into the Bounty programme - the first co-operation with Honda and a move which probably saved the company.

A £70 million press shop, new body assembly plant, paint shop and final assembly lines were built at Cowley to manufacture the Triumph Acclaim - the last Triumph-badged car - which was a twin of the Honda Ballade. The first of the 133,626 cars was built six months

August 1981 - the site is sold for £5million and the bulldozers move in, though some of the structure of the factory remains

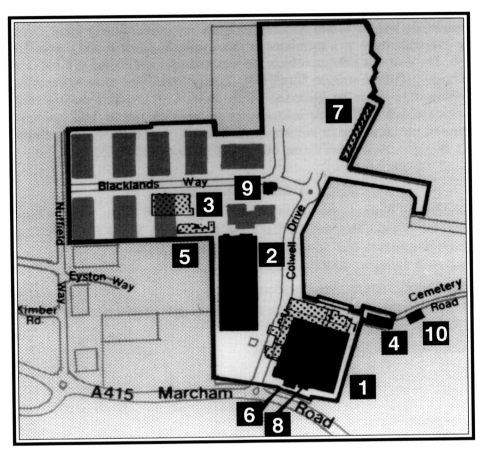

The MG factory superimposed on the layout of the Abingdon business park.
1. A-block, now re-clad, which housed the main assembly area.
2. B-block, also re-clad, which housed the tyre fitting bay, competition department, despatch, final inspection, paint repair ovens, rectification shop and design and development.
3. C. block - demolished - export despatch and special tuning.
4. Administration block - 'top office'.
5. Site of the air pollution centre, built in 1967.
6. Surgery and personnel.
7. Crash testing rig.
8. Telephone exchange. The MG Car Company's number was Abingdon 251, which also identified the first chassis number of new model runs.
9. Commemorative plaque.
10. MG Car Club office; this information is reproduced with the Club's kind permission.

after the MG factory closed, and the plan to use the site as an export packing and parts storage area was abandoned.

Abingdon was sold to an insurance company and much of the works demolished to make way for an industrial park, though the adminstration block remains and the main A and B blocks have been re-clad. However, the MG name lives on as, in 1990, Abingdon became home to head office of the MG Car Club.

Back to business

Over the years, there appeared MG badge-engineered models, like the Farina Magnettes and versions of saloons like the Austin 1100, the Maestro, Montego and the Metro. But the MGB itself began to come back to life in the

The Heritage MGB is welded together at Faringdon. The nose section is on the left.

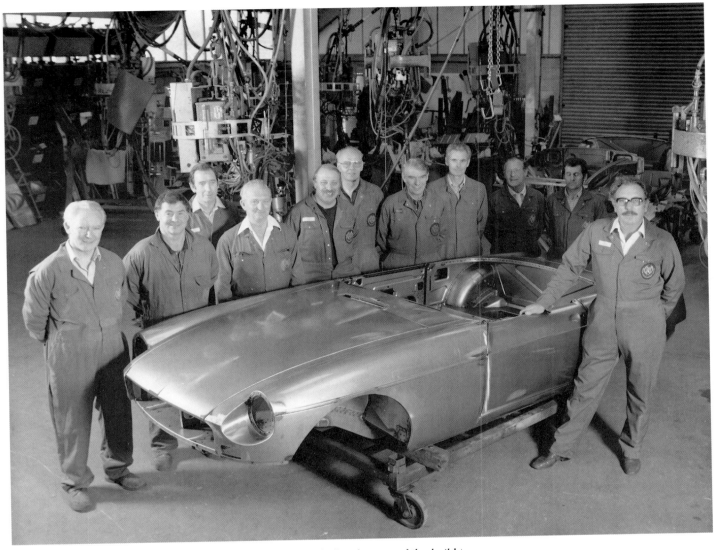

The completed shell with some of the build team.

late 80s. In 1988, the unprecedented public affection for the car, and the need to replace ageing, rust-ridden bodies, led to the production of new shells from the original tooling.

Factory sites at Oxford, Swindon and all over the Midlands were scoured for the press tools and eventually several thousand, weighing an average of a ton each, were assembled. Production was restarted at a new factory in the small Oxfordshire town of Faringdon by a new company - British Motor Heritage, a Rover group subsidiary - using many workers who had been involved with producing the cars at Abingdon.

The venture was very successful, producing, by the mid-nineties, thousands of new bodyshells for the MGB - almost all roadsters - and hundreds for the Midget. This led to demands for complete cars to be made again, which resulted, in 1990, to two prototype V8 cars being built by BMH.

The company's executive director, David Bishop, said the first was more or less knocked up in a lock-up garage; even so, its performance was stunning. When it was assessed by Rover's special projects division, it was decided to put it into production in 1992 as the MG RV8 with a limited production run of

2000 cars.

The project was codenamed PR4, and part of its function was to keep the MG name before the public while work was going on in secret on the completely new MGF, which would not be ready for another three years. So the B was reborn, with a wider track, integrated bumpers and a raised bonnet.

"There was this red herring", said David Bishop "that Abingdon had never built a V8 roadster because the 'rubber bumper' bodyshell was not rigid enough torsionally, but our 'rubber bumper' shells were near enough identical to the original chrome bumper ones [in

79

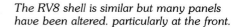
The RV8 shell is similar but many panels have been altered. particularly at the front.

strength] because weld performance is so much better now."

There was, however, considerable development work done on the shell, changing the underframe substantially to take the power of the Rover 3946cc unit, which then put out 190bhp at 4750rpm, giving a top speed of 136mph and a 0-60 time of 5.9 seconds. Almost all the panels were changed in some respect, particularly in the frontal area which required reshaped wings to take the wider track.

BMH pressed 80% of the zinc-coated panels at Faringdon, Abbey Panels made the wings and Rover's Swindon plant manufactured the doors, bonnet and bootlid. Building the shell took 27 man-hours, six more than for an MGB, after which it was painted at Cowley alongside standard production cars like the Rover 600 and 800.

Shell and mechanics were mated at Cowley in an area described as 'MG Manufacturing'. Eighteen workers hand-assembled the cars, pushing them from station to station (just like at Abingdon, but spending up to two and a half hours at each stage rather than a few minutes), and passing their own work without inspectors.

The body arrived wrapped in plastic and at the first stage there was a wax injection into the sills and other areas. The second stage was when the wiring loom was installed and the third the installation of the dash and some of the trim.

The fuel lines and tank were installed next, then the shell was lifted and dropped on to its suspension components on the axle tables. Next came the

Making MGs

Finishing touches for the RV8 shell before it is plastic-wrapped and despatched to Cowley.

insertion of the V8 engine, brake lines, radiator, steering and exhaust, then final trimming and oil and brake fluid. Each car was reviewed in a test bay for any defects and finally given a traditional MG road test.

Production rates were tiny by Abingdon standards - some 20 cars a week.

The car has proved particularly popular in Germany and Japan, where many examples - with added air conditioning - were sold.

The Rover V8 engine in modern EFI form waits in its crate. This unit was first used in an MG in 1972.

Above: Front suspension assembly about to be attached in the MG area at Cowley.

A hoist lifts the engine for installation on the elevated line.

Final trim and adjustments.

Three RV8s ready for road testing. Models destined for Japan were badged 'Rover' on the sides, as well as 'MG'.

MG for the 21st century

At the Geneva Motor Show in March 1995, 70 years after the first acknowledged MG was produced, the first brand-new MG for 33 years was announced - the MGF. It is built as a proper sports car by the Rover group and is not a saloon derivative.

Work had gone on for several years on the 'Phoenix' project, as it was dubbed in 1989, the British answer to the type of sports cars the Japanese were in the process of producing, like the Mazda MX5 and Toyota MR2.

The mid-engined MG EX-E concept car shown at the Frankfurt Motor Show in 1985 was taken as the basis for the new car, though there had been several prototypes built with different drive configurations, such as front-engine-rear-drive, like the MGB and front-wheel drive, but the mid-engined layout was better for weight distribution. Involved were 120 prototype test engines, two million test miles and 50,000 test-bed hours. All the track testing was done at night for secrecy.

The new car, eventually codenamed

At the Motor Panels Coventry factory the jig-mounted MGF is welded.

Making MGs

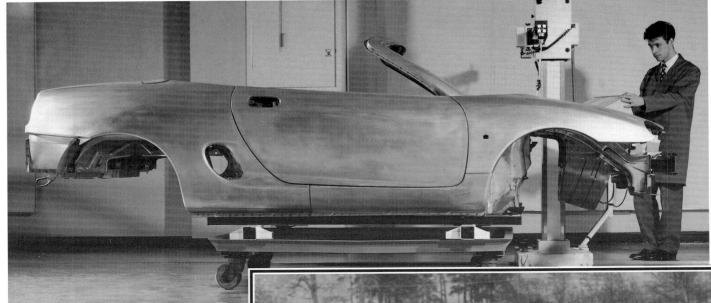

The MGF body is checked on a computerised co-ordinate table, which measures its dimensions.

PR3, has a brand-new engine - the 1800cc version of the successful Rover K-series, mounted transversely and driving the rear wheels. One version puts out 118bhp at 5500rpm, and the hotter version, with variable valve control, 143bhp at 7000rpm. This system, developed by Rover, keeps inlet valves open for longer at engine speeds above 4000rpm. Engine capacity, at 1796cc, is two cc less than the faithful B-series in the MGB, which developed 95bhp at 5400rpm.

Rover quotes speeds for the standard version as being 0-60 in 8.5 seconds with a maximum of 120mph, and the VVC model at 7.0 seconds to 60mph with a maximum of 130mph.

The original styling exercise was created by MGA Developments of Coventry and refined by Styling International. Final design of the production version was done at Rover's styling studios at Canley in Coventry. Rover manufactured the press tools, but the body engineering and production is done by Motor Panels of Coventry, who have invested £20million in the project. Motor Panels press the zinc-coated panels and

Below & overleaf: The proud successor - the MGF 1.8i - the first new MG for 33 years. Styling echoes from the past include the cream instrument dials inscribed 'MG'.

assemble the shell, which is then taken to the Longbridge plant in Birmingham for painting and mechanics.

The shell is dropped on to Metro subframes, which use Hydragas suspension. Developed more than 30 years ago by Alex Moulton, this system has been used on millions of cars.

An "appropriate degree of handwork" is employed in the car's production, says Rover.

Initial production plans, according to *Autocar,* are for 15,000 cars a year, rising to 30,000.

And why MGF? Logically, it should be the MGD, but Rover said that this appellation was given to a prototype successor to the MGB which got no further than a wooden mock-up, and the MGE was the EX-E concept car shown at the Frankfurt Motor Show in 1985.

Appendix I
Production figures

MGA PRODUCTION

Year	1500	Twin-cam	1600	1600 II	Total
1955	1003				1003
1956	13410				13410
1957	20571				20571
1958	16122	541			16663
1959	7644	1519	14156		23319
1960		51	16930		16981
1961			415	5670	6085
1962				3049	3049
Total	58,750	2111	31,501	8719	101,081

MAGNETTE PRODUCTION

Year	ZA	ZB	Total
1953	8		8
1954	3819		3819
1955	8927		8927
1956	5322	2063	7385
1957		6910	6910
1958		9551	9551
Total	18,076	18,524	36,600

MG Y-TYPE SALOON AND TOURER PRODUCTION

Year	YA	YT	YB	Total
1947	923			923
1948	1048	43		1091
1949	1383	586		1969
1950	1827	248		2075
1951	977		16	993
1952			722	722
1953			563	563
Total	6158	877	1301	8336

MGB/C/V8 PRODUCTION

Year	MGB		MGC		V8	Total
	Tourer	GT	Tourer	GT	GT	
1962	4518					4518
1963	23308					23308
1964	26542					26542
1965	24179	524				24703
1966	22675	10241	9	4		32929
1967	15128	11396	182	38		26744
1968	17355	8352	2596	2491		30794
1969	18887	12135	1757	1925		34704
1970	23662	12510				36172
1971	22511	12169				34680
1972	26222	13171			3	39396
1973	19546	10208			1070	30824
1974	19757	9626			853	30236
1975	20171	4517			482	25170
1976	25527	3656			183	29366
1977	24483	4198				28681
1978	21702	5652				27354
1979	19897	3503				23400
1980	10891	3424				14315
sub-total	386,961	125,282	4544	4458	2591	
Total	512,243		9002		2591	523,836

MIDGET PRODUCTION

Year	Mark I	Mark II	Mark III	1500	Total
1961	7656				7656
1962	9906				9906
1963	7625				7625
1964	494	10956			11450
1965		9162			9162
1966		6483	359		6842
1967			7854		7854
1968			7272		7272
1969			12965		12965
1970			15106		15106
1971			16469		16469
1972			16243		16243
1973			14048		14048
1974			9930	2513	12443
1975				14478	14478
1976				16879	16879
1977				14329	14329
1978				14312	14312
1979				9778	9778
Total	25,681	26,601	100,246	72,289	224,817

In 1967, some 470 Midgets were produced at Cowley for reasons which have not been adequately explained. Abingdon also produced 129,362 Austin-Healey Sprites, the Austin-Healey 3000, the Riley RM series and Pathfinder, Morris Minor Travellers, vans and pick-ups and the Vanden Plas 1500.

MG SPORTS CAR PRODUCTION 1946-1980

Year	TC	TD	TF	MGA	MGB	MGC	Midget	GTV8	Total
1945	81								81
1946	1675								1675
1947	2346								2346
1948	3085								3085
1949	2813	98							2911
1950		4767							4767
1951		7451							7451
1952		10838							10838
1953		6510	1620						8130
1954			6520						6520
1955			1460	1003					2463
1956				13410					13410
1957				20571					20571
1958				16663					16663
1959				23319					23319
1960				16981					16981
1961				6085			7656		13741
1962				3049	4518		9906		17473
1963					23308		7625		30933
1964					26542		11450		37992
1965					24703		9162		33865
1966					32916	13	6482		39771
1967					26524	220	7854		38298
1968					25707	5087	7272		38066
1969					31022	3682	12965		47669

(continued)

MG SPORTS CAR PRODUCTION 1946-1980 *(continued)*									
Year	TC	TD	TF	MGA	MGB	MGC	Midget	GTV8	Total
1970					36172		15106		51278
1971					34680		16469		51149
1972					39393		16243	3	55639
1973					29754		14048	1070	44872
1974					29383		12443	853	42679
1975					24688		14478	482	39648
1976					29183		16879	183	46245
1977					28681		14329		43010
1978					27354		14312		41666
1979					23400		9778		33178
1980					14315				
Total	10,000	29,664	9600	101,081	512,243	9002	224,817	2591	898,988

Appendix II
Bibliography

Great Marques - MG Chris Harvey (Octopus 1983)

MG Companion Kenneth Ullyet (Stanley Paul 1960)

MG Mania (The Insomnia Crew) Henry W Stone (New England MG T Register 1983)

MGA Robert Vitrikas (Scarborough Fair 1980)

MGA Wilson McComb (Osprey 1983)

MGA, MGB and MGC Graham Robson (MRP 1978)

MGB- Illustrated History Wood & Burrell (G T Foulis 1988)

Original MGA Anders Clausager (Bay View Books 1993)

Original MGB Anders Clausager (Bay View Books 1994)

Original Sprite and Midget Terry Horler (Bay View Books 1994)

The A B and C Chris Harvey (Oxford Illustrated Press 1980)

The Art of Abingdon John McLellan (MRP 1980)

The MG Collection Richard Monk (PSL 1994)

The MG Story Anders Clausager (G T Foulis 1982)

The T-series MGs Graham Robson (MRP 1981)

Bound volumes: *Motor Sport, Classic and Sportscar, Classic Cars, Autocar, Motor, Safety Fast, Oxford Mail.*

Index

Making MGs